Gay Poem lands like a necessary spanking we all need—especially if we have ever participated in the lazy, inherited rhetoric or stereotypes that diminish others. This collection of poems is a display of personal excavation and course correction. A lowercase declaration of truth that sparkles loudly for rainbow justice. A work of divine alchemy, transmuting righteous anger into revelation and holy shame into invitation.

"Listen closely," Ameer Drane writes, "and you can hear the guttural screams of my intrusive thoughts and prayers." A raw vulnerability pulses throughout this book. It is uncomfortable, confronting, and ultimately liberating.

— Gabriela Moriarty, Bangkok Poet and Artist

From begging for others to "Validate me" to insisting they "Deal with it," this book charts the path to radical self-love in a world of cheap thrills, digital commodification, and objectification that devalues and constricts the Self into the forgettable little boxes Pete Seeger sang about. It's as much a self-reflective journey of transformation as an inward focused cultural critique that shows us a shattered self cannot rebuild the shattered world around them.

Many of these poems have also stood the test of the crucible that is the Bangkok Poetry Slam, multiple times over! Ameer is undeniably talented in his writing, how he frames his story and message, and the way he delivers each poem when performing at the mic!

— Pableroy, Director of Bangkok Lyrical Lunacy

Gay Poem is an amazing collection of poems and prose exploring the unique intersection of being gay and Black in current times. Ameer Drane is a voice to be reckoned with. If you're already into poetry, you'll love his work; if you're getting back into poetry, you'll find something in this book that will resonate with you and leave you wanting to read and hear more.

— Frederick Smith, Author of *One and Done* and *Love is a Contact Sport*

Inspiring and important in the current political climate. *Gay Poem* is a testament to Queer empowerment. These poems will resonate with so many queer people. Thank you, Ameer, for being a voice for so many queer individuals and allowing our truth to be heard.

— Nunoy van den Burgh, Choreographer, Model, and Creative Producer

A powerful reflection on the gay experience and what it looks like to liberate ourselves through acceptance of our gifts as much as our shadows. I never expected a book of poetry to capture so artfully the trials, hopes, and tribulations of my 20's, from the dance floors to the quiet days after. These poems make parts of me flinch and then soften at finally feeling understood and held at the same time.

— Craig Cassey, Sex & Relationship Coach

Gay Poem asks a question most poets won't touch: what does it actually feel like to inhabit a queer Black body in relation to other queer men's bodies? Drane doesn't look away—from the longing, the objectification, or the ambivalence about both.

— Dr. Ryan M. Kull, Psychoanalyst

Gay Poem is a revelation; each poem charts the author's perspective navigating the queer Black experience. His loneliness, heartbreak, and hypersexuality reflect how one copes in a fetishized ecosystem, ultimately reclaiming these aspects as proud, self-assured, and sensual. Ameer's debut highlights the emergence of a new poetic voice poised to cement itself among the greats.

— Lisa Wills, Writer and Founder of Knicname Films

Ameer Drane is a poet, writer, and spoken word performance artist from Milwaukee, Wisconsin, USA.

He has a bachelor's degree in Romance Languages and Literatures from the University of Chicago and a master's degree in Spanish Linguistics from the University of California, Los Angeles.

Ameer's poetry reflects on the intersections of gay hookup culture, queer identity, race, social media, mental health, and American politics.

Now based in Bangkok, Thailand, Ameer is an active member of the city's poetry scene. He is a regular guest host of the Lyrical Lunacy poetry events and a three-time winner of the Bangkok Poetry Slam.

Gay Poem is his debut poetry collection.

GAY POEM

AMEER DRANE

aedrane
poetry

ISBN: 9798993802701

Cover design by Aaron McMillan

Author photo by Ark Saroj

Published by Ameer Drane

First Edition

For permissions or inquiries, visit www.gaypoem.com.

For Sheba, Dawn, and Chew Meng

CONTENTS

The place in which I fit will not exist until I make it.

- JAMES BALDWIN

GAY POEM

ACT ONE

looking for?

SUCK IT

being a poet is so fucking embarrassing.

the other gays are always like, *here's a self-
deprecating joke about how much I love
sucking dick, haha.* & I'm like, *here's a self-
reflective poem about how much I hate
pretending it feels good to suppress the non-
sexual parts of myself, haha. do you
still wanna suck my dick or...*

what?

MUSCLE BOI

validate me.

tell me that you love me because my body is sexy, that you are fucking obsessed, that you can't be expected to control yourself around me.

devour me.

quantify my worth by how much you want to fuck me. my skin: your fantasy. my body: built to be used, built to pull the attention of men.

your gaze

liberates me from ever feeling like a worthless gay boy again. so, give me it all: your fire, your likes, your heart-eye emojis. right now. I'm

begging you.

please! I need it. you know I'm just a mindless muscle boi. no thoughts, no feelings. just horny, endlessly. waiting to be chosen, consumed: all

for you. your praise, incessant lust—it's like currency. each compli-
ment bringing me closer to buying that pride the community shop

only sells

to the fit, fuckable gays. you're making me rich! how can I repay you?
a flirtatious wink? on demand access to nudes? silence as you grab

my dick

without consent while passing me at the bar? anything, babe. look at
me. I'm asking for it. I'm barely a human. I'm 50% off. subscribe. link

in bio.

JUNGLE FEVER

superhuman
dominant
sexual
force
of nature

your skin
color is hot
your naked
body excites
your black
cock matters

your intellect
your safety
your emotions
are of interest
to no one

BIG BLACK

fuck your fantasy.
fuck your request for measurements.
fuck your audacity to call anyone a *bbc*.
fuck your *jungle fever*—I hope it fucking burns.
fuck your preference for objectification.
fuck your can't separate porn from reality—you lazy fuck.
fuck your *black dicks matter*.
fuck your jokes disguised as solidarity.
fuck your privilege.
fuck your casual racism.
fuck your *but I'm [insert ethnicity]*—yea,
fuck you, too.
fuck your insensitivity.
fuck your lack of empathy.
fuck your *it's a compliment*—it's not, you fucking idiot.
fuck your refusal to apologize so you don't have to feel bad.
fuck your fight to remain ignorant.
fuck your *but that other black guy didn't care.*
fuck your race play.
fuck your thinking we're all the same.

for all the guys you've treated like objects, slaves to your fetish,
replaceable sex machines: fuck you.

maybe they didn't tell you. maybe they didn't have the energy to care.
maybe they brushed off whatever dumbass thing you said 'cause

you're not worth the fucking trouble.

but here's something to remember the next time you see them or me:
you're not a *size queen.*

you're the court jester, a clown—making yourself look like a fucking
joke, bigger than any *big black cock* could ever be.

fuck you.

THOSE NUDES

I.
you gotta send those nudes
again. this fucking app keeps losing
my messages. yet, every time I try
to delete it, I'm pulled back by a
dick
pic. face pic. then a
hole. new message. can't go. not yet. he's
hot. wants to meet. looks
like...have we fucked? I'll never forget
those nudes.

II.
your profile says you're looking for
friends and fun. yea,
right! emphasis on the
word *fun*. only wanna be
friends when the benefits make your
throat
gag. heart skip. toes

curl. thighs shake. eyes roll. oh,
fuck...what's your name? I'll never forget
those nudes.

III.
where are you, my *friend?* my body craves
touch from someone who wants,
but doesn't need,
to fuck. someone who sees this app is the one
fucking us. even if we delete it,
it knows how to make us
come
back. inside our minds, controlling our fucking
lives...forever? I'll never forget
those nudes.

felt cute. might fuck around and find out if I want more
than: horny? hung? hot. hey. how are you? good. wanna
fuck? tomorrow. tonight. now. today. more pics? yea,
you? not my type. fuck you. you're arrogant. ugly. gross.
blocked. how much? please. I'll pay. hey there. hey boy.
hey daddy. sexy. fuck. you top? bottom? nice. how big?
uncut? show me. your. big. black. cock. hole. face. pic.
wow. hey. looking? for fun. for now. for any. party. play.
group. high. hey. clean? on prep. me too. where are you?
so close. hey. into? no fats. no fems. no drama. only masc.
muscular. manly. men. ok. no strings. no kissing. no names.
just preference. just raw. just fun. this is fun. isn't it? was it?
don't know. felt horny. felt bored. felt lonely. felt stressed.
felt cute? might delete. feel trapped. redownload later.

A SIP

he had the depth of an ocean, but he couldn't resist the hypnotic
trance of the shallow hot boys' siren song.

your waters are much too dark and tumultuous to swim, they sang.
no one will ever risk drowning in someone like you.

can you try being smaller, lighter, easier to control and contain?
then we can teach you how to be one of us.

start by becoming what we need tonight: a bottle of water.
yes, be plastic, cold, easy to have 'fun'

with a little x or g. then all the boys will wanna take
a sip. oceans are boring, but tonight

we can make you a star
of the after

party.

I wanted the hot boys to think I was one of them; so, I showed them my muscles and masculinity. I wanted the intellectuals to think I was one of them, too; so, I covered my body and showed them my critical thinking skills and university degrees. I wanted the people who felt rejected by the hot boys and the intellectuals to know I still felt like one of them, too; so, I covered my body, simplified my thoughts, and showed them my humor and empathy. it all worked for a while— until everyone could sense it: I only wanted their acceptance to hide how insecure I felt about accepting me for me.

the sex was amazing, and
tonight I'll tell my friends
while carefully hiding
the next day was awful.

I'll bottle that feeling,
deliver it to my therapist,
pouring its contents unfiltered
onto her office floor as I recall:

the sex was amazing, but,
once again, I lost myself
inside of him or outside of
me—I don't know for sure.

but, I do know,
at the climax of feeling
the sweat...the rush...the release...
everything I thought I was craving,

I could hear that lonely boy crying:
this isn't what I asked for.
this was escaping, temporarily.
this will never be where we find home.

she'll repeat it all back to me
before digging deeper into why
the sex was amazing, but
the next day was awful.

THE WORDS I DIDN'T KNOW THEN

I wish we could go back in time and

eat my silence.

I'd take all my unspoken *ifs*, *whats*, and *hows*,

chop them into tiny squares,

and make an omelette just how you like.

the setting sun

would filter through

your kitchen blinds,

drawing golden lines

down my bare back,

                              and you'd sneak behind to kiss

                the tender spot of my neck

somehow only you could find.

                           opening your fridge,

                I'd discover an expired

                           carton of eggs.

I'll go buy some, I'd say,

                  laughing softly

while struggling to find

                  the hole for my head

                           in your favorite t-shirt.

with clothes finally on,

                  I'd head out, knowing

                           I'd soon return to undress

                  myself with you

                           all over again.

the mischief in your eyes

as you wave goodbye

would linger within,

sending me deep into a salacious daydream,

until a heavy sigh from

the corner store cashier

brings me back to reality.

but, as you know,

that's not the way

things go.

there was no omelette,

no returning,

no mischief in your eyes,

just sorrow:

the bitter realization that

you'd never want

to see me again.

years later,

those eyes still haunt me,

      following me wherever I go,

              slicing me open like

      a sleep-deprived surgeon

with a butter knife,

    ruthlessly dragging the dull blade across the soft skin below

             my adam's apple,

    determined to finally give way

to the words I didn't know then

      how to say:

             I believe you.
             I need time to process, but
             this doesn't change how I feel.

             thank you for letting me know
             undetectable equals
             untransmittable.

AGAIN SOON

fully booked, the clinic on
a rough sunday morning
as the pigs and bears
and otters and cruisers
and lovers and losers
and teachers and students
and writers and poets
and plumbers and painters
and lawyers and bankers
and actors and waiters
and hosts and holes
just for
lonely
big
dick
men
pretend we give a fuck
about the doctor
telling us to be
safe.

turn on the fucking news,
doc. none of us are *safe*
here.

just give us the meds,
so, at least, we may
fuck again soon.

HIGH RISK (PRE-EXPOSURE)

high risk sexual behavior—that's your problem, the doctor says,
judgmentally, igniting a fire in the pit of my chest. I want to yell,

you stupid bitch! what does 'high risk' even mean?! but I don't.
because I know. I've been high risk all my life. high risk on

playgrounds, running to avoid the boys threatening to bury my
head in the concrete. high risk walking home, hoping the word

faggot would be the only thing to hit me in the face. high risk
speaking up with a voice that sounds *too gay.* high risk holding

hands. high risk showing affection for too long. high risk at work,
at school, at home, at the doctor, in churches, on the train, online,

on the street—anywhere, anytime. it's easy to be high risk when
you're someone like me. it always has been. so, with dead eyes,

I accept the little blue pills that won't stop my life from being risky.
but they will reduce the risks I take while hiding inside the voids

of other *high risk* men. together, in unison, without knowing each other's names, we'll feel...*safe*...connected...seen...able to forget

for a moment all the risks we take while navigating a world still trying to punish us...for being...surviving...for loving freely.

ACT TWO

are you

WILD

why am I still afraid
of being called *wild?*
for it is true: I am
made by the divine
to be the human boy
form of the sun...sea...
rivers...flow...flowers...

WHY DO SOME GAY MEN HATE
GAY MEN WHO ARE FEMININE?

when I was a little boy, my maternal grandmother
told my mother to slap me right across the face
whenever I said or did any of that *girly shit*.

my mother refused to hit me—thank god.
she was beaten as a child and couldn't stand
the thought of doing the same to me.

of course, she never stopped worrying about
someone else hitting me first. and they did—
each time reminding her of just how hard
my life would be (heartbreak for a mother).

now, I can imagine that if that first strike to my
face came from the woman who I loved most,
maybe I'd have grown up to fear and then also
hate any *girly shit* being around or within me.

some say hurt people hurt people.

I guess the hurting hurts a little
less when you get to be the one who
slaps someone else's face for a change.

OF SWEET SPRING

lilac bloom, soft sun
alluring breeze, warm in heart
of sweet spring, you are...

- TO MY INNER CHILD

you...you are the boy who feels too much for his own good
(or so they say).
you who stares up at the crisp white clouds and dreams.
you who doesn't mind if that toy is supposedly for girls
and that one is for boys.
you are fantastic, ecstatic magic (yes, you are).
you are that smile revealing all those big, beautiful teeth.
you talk funny (you sure do).
you laugh loud (yes, it's true).
you are too grand to be put in a teeny little box.
you who runs so fast you can't feel the soles of your feet.
you are sunshine on a december afternoon.
you are a whimsical boy (yes, indeed).
you are golden brown perfection baked in a gentle heat.
you are the adventure your mother prayed for.
you are the moment your family has been pushing toward.
you are right on time, last in line but the first to sip, swirl,
swish, slurp, and swallow a splash of life's sweet bliss.

you are chosen—not by another person but by that voice
that sings inside of you.
you are the song.
you are the rhythm.
you are the beat.
you are everything, every feeling that you have ever needed
to be...you.

PROTECT THE CHILDREN
(IN YOUR NAME)

protect the children, my lord, my savior. teach them
hatred with love. inject their imaginations with a
devotion to never being enough. for you, make them
fear, submit. no questions, no wonder. to follow, they
need to fold, to cower, to shake, to learn the laws of
men. the rules, they must obey. the hell, they must
~~create!~~ avert. the heathens, they must ~~conquer!~~
convert. protect them from the communists, and
the woke, and the muslims, and the jews. from
the feminists, and the gays, and the trans, and
the liberals spreading fake news! docile innocence
now plagued. family values at stake. theories too
critical for fragile minds to take! the children,
protect. you must. my lord, my savior, I beg.
I pray to you. mine! the bible says, the bible
cries, the bible screams! torture. glory! suffer.
believe! cleanse. repent! terror. oh, please!
protect them. give them faith in me, faith in
my word as your word, my fear as your fear,

my hate as your hate! in your name! in my
image! my lord! my savior! my god! mine!
mine! mine! amen. me.

HOW THE WORLD LIMITS US

streets uncertain
safety reduced to bars and clubs
can't have the love you desire
or
the love you lost
prove your worth to god
they say he hates you
read the signs
read the room
read the laws
read these bitches to filth
you don't belong here
your lifestyle is disgusting
a disgrace to this family
no one wants to see that shit
withhold everything that makes you feel joy
swallow every man that makes you feel joy
who's your daddy?
face down

ass up
arch your back
more
even more
nice
now, be a good boy and
listen: the clinic called
turns out you are
just a hole and,
for some ungodly reason,
brunch is reserved for fucking father's
day, at 11:11 pm, so
remember to
look both ways before you
go to hell, and
don't you dare think about running
to that country
or that town
or that neighborhood
or that street
or that...
wait, are you high?
you know you could be stoned
lynched
jailed
beaten
to pulp
hunted
for sport
picked last
for the team
with your
limp wrists

chicken legs
two left feet
like a girl, you run, boy
not so fast now are you, boy?
put your hands above your head, boy
you have the right to remain in line, boy
don't give a fuck if it's on camera, boy
your name, just another hashtag, boy
now, did I make myself clear, boy?
I said, did I make myself clear, boy?!
can't breathe, boy
can't be, boy
can't, boy
( ), boy?
policed by men who don't see you as human
cruised by men who don't see you as human
fucked by men who don't see you as human
are you sure you're even a human?
the bible says you're a pig
a cow
a chicken
a cock
a pussy
a lion
a tiger
a bear
stuffed with semen
behind the bush
in the shadow
through the hole
at the gym
on a whim
just be hot for fuck's sake

like that guy on x
(formerly twitter)
the go-go boy at the circuit party
the dom top looking for now
the fresh meat on PrEP
c'mon, please, I'm begging you, please
let me see that big fat blackity black black dick
now a face pic
for a hole pic
any more pics?
took a new pic
hot, right?
body-ody
body goals
body count
one, two, three, four, five, six, seven,
eight pack
chiseled chest
thick back
boulder shoulders
smell my pits
spit in my mouth
cum on my face
masc guys only
masc muscular guys only
masc-muscular-manly-straight-acting-down-low-no-sissy-
drug-and-disease-free-clean guys only
you're cute though
not enough though
never enough
never never
never enough
never
for me,

you will never be enough
look at you
look at me, now
look, buying that sandwich is homophobic
bro, eating that sandwich will make you fat
wow, smelling that sandwich is making me horny
is that a symptom of chlamydia
or am I tripping
balls?
dude, what the fuck is wrong with you?!
fucking faggot
fucking fairy
fucking groomer
fucking homo
fucking cock sucking bitch ass gay nigga
fuck fuck fuck
fuck, you are so hot
fuck, you are gorgeous
fuck, you wanna fuck me?
fuck, can I fuck you?
fuck, yea
fuck, man
fuck, no
fucking hell
fucking asshole
fucking dick
fuck off
fuck it, let's fucking fuck
fuckkkkkkkkkk, you feel goooooooooood

the voices rattle the cage
eyes open to flickering white lights
a whisper echoes across the chamber

escape

escape

escape

escape

escape.

STAINS

history be **stained**

                            stolen land: free

red rum beginnings

                            white hoods haunt

blue bombs delivered

                            stars, *en masse*, shoot

make a wish for the

                            brown, broke, and black

pledge allegiance

                            stains still there

oh say, can you

                    see the **stains**?

peek underneath   42

                  the welcome mat

no place like home

                  oh say, I can't

unsee 'em no more

                    stains

                                    everywhere

                    stains

listen closely, and you can hear the guttural screams of my
intrusive thoughts
and prayers. they tell me to smile and do a little twirl so you
can see the carpet

burns tattooed on the caps of my knees, the hungry hickeys
sucking my shoulder
blades, and the scar on my neck from that one time I almost
swallowed a bear

trap I found in a bottom's second hole. bless his heart! he had
a good heart and
a nice hole, too. but body language bewilders me. so, if you're
gonna choke me,

choke me like you mean it or don't at all. every night, I pray
to god my big black
cock doesn't burn off before the next insurrection. can't let
this country go down

on me in flames. did I ever tell you your dad jerked off to my
onlyfans in a day-
dream I had while eating kumamoto oysters and tripping on
five grams of magic

mushrooms? it. was. so. hot. is he still single? if so, tell him
I don't have an
onlyfans, but I do write poems about being an african-
american faggot who

is an intellectual, muscle boi slut and a feral fucking dog
running laps around
the public school that feeds the state prison. eight minutes
and forty-six seconds is

my personal best. fuck the police! and, for the record, I eat
all my lemons whole
instead of bitching about the cost of having somewhere to
shit. defecating with

dignity is for paying customers only. but my piss does smell
like sweet and sour
pork when I sob in the handicap bathroom stall at work. yum!
some say sex work

is work. I could never. my dick is too shy. bless the brave, rock-
hard dicks among
us. I'm gonna gargle boiling holy water to cleanse this rotted
brain. until then,

consider me a sassy pirouette of smoke coming from the
dankest weed in fake
freedom land. I puff my black chest and flow through
warm mouths daily.

don't take me too seriously. I kid. then, I adult. it's another
monday on the goddamn
clock, and I am just so fucking sick and tired and high
on everything—but life.

you know, sometimes I just wanna write saved in the hidden folder
poetry. you can only read one poem at a time 'cause I don't know

what the fuck is on the next page poetry. can't let you read it in public
'cause it's just too damn disrespectful and nasty poetry. gotta make

sure it's safe in here poetry. you know what I mean poetry. it's like,
what are you doing poetry? you looking for fun poetry? what are

you into poetry? you like it rough, don't you poetry? are you on
PrEP poetry? then, come get this load poetry. oh, oh, oh poetry!

conservatives are gonna hate me poetry. they'll say this shit is that
can't say *faggot*, so let's just call it *groomer* poetry. that *gay agenda*

poetry. that possessed by the goddamn devil himself poetry. oh well
poetry. they were never gonna accept me poetry. with their keyboards

in the middle of the night, they're gonna come for me poetry. well,
I say, *cum for me* poetry. I can take it poetry. want me to beg like a

good little boy for basic human rights and respect from you poetry?
well, fuck you poetry. I'm a human being just like you poetry. and

I'm not always this vulgar poetry. just refuse to hide my humanity
for your comfort poetry. you ever wonder why we're like this poetry?

maybe it's because, as kids, we were fed the idea that there was
something wrong with us poetry. got pushed around on the play-

ground poetry. adults looked the other way, told us to *toughen up*
poetry. *stop crying like a little girl*, they said poetry. *god hates fags*,

they said poetry. *you're going straight to hell*, they said poetry. then,
they decided it was better to pretend we don't exist poetry. made us

scared to be seen out in public poetry. forced us to hide poetry. might
get attacked on the street poetry. might get sent to jail poetry. might

get fired from your job poetry. disowned by your family poetry. lose
everything you have poetry. and they said this *lifestyle* is a choice

poetry. said we can get sick and die poetry. said we'd be getting what
we deserve poetry. so, if my sexuality makes you uncomfortable,

I don't give a fuck anymore poetry. I don't need your approval to be
alive poetry. I am gay poetry. I am queer poetry. I am black poetry.

I am soft poetry. I am muscular poetry. I am intellectual, ethical
slut poetry. not gonna let you put me in a box poetry. yes, I have

sexual desires poetry! yes, I still thrive poetry! yes, I still cry poetry!
and still I rise poetry! I follow in the footsteps of fucking legends

poetry! at least, I'm going to try poetry. because we're all going to die poetry. yes, I said, *die* poetry! so, you can either fuck off or watch me

turn it all into poetry...poetry...poetry!

ACT THREE

hey, what

HOLD ON

sweat forms between each crevice, each
line. I tremble and squeeze tight. babe, I
love
you, but these rough hands of mine are
terrified, tormented, trapped rewinding
greedy
memories of all the men like us beaten
purple and ink blue. perhaps pink
hearts
on their sleeves still, but, jaded, they
now walk these streets with a crusty
apprehension:
our loving hands out must fight to hold

on.

you could put our bodies in a box and
leave them out to rot on the side of the road.
you can ban our books, restrict our art, and say
it's to *protect the children* you know you don't
give a fuck about. you can detest our presence,
despise our resilience, resent our courage to
achieve things you couldn't even dream of.
we're used to it. numb, we know it's easier
to attack the vulnerable than to come to
terms with the fact that you're scared: not
of god, or drag queens, or transgender people,
or who uses which bathroom. you're scared of
how much our expression of love for ourselves
and each other reveals you only truly know hate.
what rules must you obey to receive even an
imitation of affection? are those chains around
your necks still symbols of your devotion or
domestication? you filthy animals! how is it
still possible you can't see? if you killed us

all tonight, put our bodies in a box, left us out
to rot on the side of the road, the next morning,
before the sun rises, one of you would give birth to
our next generation because you will never eradicate
our light.

sweet lotus flower, starved
of light,
you are not alone,
with young roots torn
from wretched soil,
please cling to the mud
of my grief,
please disturb the peace
of my morning,
please curl into the vigor
of my vines,
hide not in deprivation,
let me ease your trepidation,
I'll affirm without hesitation,
you were not born
to drown.

you, too, are destined
to bathe
in the glorious rays

of a gentle sun,
you, too, are destined
to rise,
to blossom,
to endure & overcome,
so please, my
sweet lotus flower, worthy
of light,
do not let these
desolate waters
convince you to wither
before it is your time
to bloom.

SACRED AND ETERNAL

this morning
my eyes caught

a progress pride
flag dancing

in harsh wind
like a flame

sacred and eternal
light untamed

THE PHOENIX

your identity isn't set in stone

it's malleable

you can change

you can even self-destruct

burn to ashes

rise again

and again
and again
and again

as many times as you need

it's never too late

overlooked, undervalued, underestimated, forgotten, misunderstood, discarded, ridiculed, harassed, humiliated, bullied, laughed at, held back, pushed down, put in a box, shoved into a corner, told no, told not yet, told not ever, told to be quiet if I want people to like me, told to speak up if I want people to respect me, told to shut the fuck up, spoken over, mocked, disrespected, silenced, ignored, muted, unfollowed, blocked, ghosted, left on read, picked last, not picked because of the color of my skin, only picked because of the color of my skin, fetishized, objectified, groped, tossed aside, treated like an option of an option of an option, manipulated, made fun of by the cool kids, rejected by the misfits, called a *little bitch*, called a *faggot*, called another black guy's name because to you we're all the same, made to feel small, dangerous, lazy, weak, no good, never enough, lacking, insignificant, incapable, incompetent, incomplete...

so, if you see me shining now, just know I had to fight the voice inside that says I don't deserve to.

so, if you see me shining now, just know I had to work for each one
of these rays of light.

so, if you see me shining now, just know I had to learn that I have
always been a star.

so, no.

                                             I will not dim.

I will not tone it down.

                                        I will not hide myself.

not for you.

                                        not for anyone.

not anymore.

don't be staring at the sun for so long if you already know
you can't handle the heat.

I'll burn the whites of your eyes.

one day, you'll see.

you'll be on your knees, eyes closed, desperate arms
stretched toward storm clouds swallowing the sky.

you'll be praying for my light, praying for my warmth,
praying for my brilliance to radiate near you again.

I'll hear you pray.
I'll watch you beg.
I'll shine again
down on you
if, and only if,
I fucking feel
like it.

CRUMBS OF A CONSTELLATION

I am multidimensional by nature, by birth, by god; or so I believe.
I do believe in *something*. sometimes that *something* is me.
sometimes it is beyond me. like...

I am cosmic stardust, okay? like...I am a grown ass man who
likes to let his saturated mind leak on the keyboard, okay?
brain juice so thick the space

                              bar

                                                            got

sticky

nospacesherenomorejustwordscollectedinabucketofslop.
delicious! there it is again: that space between you
me. but the *and* got lost

in space, pulled by force, trapped in the orbit of a saturn
moon. my mind is the crumbs of the nearest constellation.
yea, bro! didn't even have to smoke

no dope, no ganja, no kush, no...mary jane loves spiderman
more than I can sink my teeth into an apple. forbidden! I am
the coldest of them all. snow black like

oil. oil slick like his dick. yes, bitch, I said, *like his dick*. we
gay here. people be gay. some people be trans, too. uh...
I don't know why you act like you got

the power to say they can't. you ain't god, now is you? so, you
don't know how they experience their lives. just like nobody
truly knows how you experience your shit

life either. consciousness is intangible, dumbass! have some
faith in his divine artistry. the binary don't exist! surely,
you know he paints in more shades than

black and white. so, stop pretending you know which colors
dance inside the heart of another. you don't, silly! you
can't, silly! you fucking dick, fucking fear-

mongering, don't-think, empathy-lacking, know-nothing
prick! oh, boy, I tell ya what. open up that mind. there's
stars out here in space. come see: the vision!

baby!

               held captive

on the dance floor

               I am

real deep in

               my hip bones

                              swingin'

               here, boys

                           free to embrace

               and shake

some ass

to hard bass

our sweaty hands

go *clap, clap*

my fingers high

gotta *snap, snap*

dj set

comin' in hot

like a sermon

got me goin'

on cloud nine

to heaven

I can hardly

stand on

these sore feet

but we gon'

keep movin'

and groovin'

to these silky

hypnotic

warehouse

ba, ba, ba

beats!

beats!

beats!

beats!

this beat got me

like jelly

I am

the music

I am

the rhythm

I am

the flow

in motion

                            I am

                                                belly

                           sweatin'

                                               hips

                           shakin'

ass

                           clappin'

heart

                           poundin'

like

                           drums!

                                             drums!

                           drums!

                                           drums!

                          boys

twerkin'

                                dj

spittin'

                             sunlight

creepin'

                               floor

                                                      crackin'

                             bliss

                                                   'til that

                             beat

done!

                             done!

done!

                             done!

                                                    my shirt off

                          feel me baby

                                                      'cause

                           this beat got

this beat got

        this beat got

                me like

jelly!

        jelly!

                jelly!

MY MOTHER'S CHOICE

while attending a fancy elite american college, I would often
lie whenever anyone would ask me about my parents' age.

oh, they had me when they were young, I'd say. *early twenty-
something* (or a random number, depending on who I was

talking to). even with some of my closest friends, I was scared to
say the truth: my mom was sixteen years old when I was born on

the twenty-fifth of april, nineteen ninety-one (just twelve days
before her seventeenth birthday). sometimes, if I felt comfortable,

I would lie and tell people she was seventeen instead of sixteen. for
some reason, the idea of her being one year away from adulthood felt

safer, like it would cause less shock or make me feel less different, less
like a mistake. I guess I was just worried people would judge me if

they found out I was born to a teenage mother. most of my classmates
were white *and/or* wealthy *and/or* had attended private schools

and/or had parents much older than my mom. I didn't want people to think I didn't belong there (which was often how I felt inside) or say

that the only reason I got into a fancy elite american college was because of affirmative action (but, I'm sure some still thought that).

now, as a thirty-four-year-old man, I look back at that version of me and feel so stupid for how much I worried about people knowing my

mom's age. at sixteen, she gave birth to me. she sacrificed a lot to raise me. after high school, she went to community college to become a

registered nurse. she has worked harder than most can fathom. she would do anything for me and my brothers. she is the reason I love

reading. she is the reason I am intelligent. she never fails to remind me of my worth. she listens to me whenever I am down. she lifts me

up. she cheers for me even when I cannot cheer for myself. she embraces me as I am. she loves me, always. sometimes I wonder

what her life might have been like, who she'd be, if she didn't have me so young. she says she believes reality is better. *this was not an*

accident, she says. *I had the right to choose, and I chose you.* these days, I tell everyone my mom had me when she was sixteen, and

I do not care who struggles to imagine being so strong.

BECAUSE I AM GOING TO DIE

because I am going to die / & I know / no one will give a fuck
how many people on instagram / thought I was hot or cool
because I no longer doubt / if I am worthy of / or good at
sex / & love / & friendship / & learning / & being human
because I stopped believing / I would find happiness
following the arbitrary rules & timeline / of a repressed society
because I will never forget / how much I hated / working so hard
to help build someone else's dream / while neglecting my own
because I cannot ignore / anymore / how there's no guarantee
that I'll still be here tomorrow / in ten minutes / or in fifty years
because whenever it is my time / I want to die knowing
I did / in a way that only I could / what I was born to do:

I lived

I lived

I lived

Black but like brown sugar
melting in a pan.

Gay as in *nigga, you so gay*
even yo' hairline ain't straight.

Soft just like garden soil
after heavy summer rain.

They say if ya dig ya nails
in my back during missionary,

work is needed to remove my clunky
residue from the depths of ya soul.

But ain't nobody got time to apologize
for shit I can't control. I was born

this way: quiet, sensitive, queer,
and fearless as fuck.

I may appear to crumble at ya feet.
But I'll ball these hands, make two

fists, clumsy, go out swingin'
if I have to. Nothin' to lose,

so best believe I'll roast ya mouth
with at least one jab, make ya see

I'm cut from that resilient
rainbow cloth.

Yes, ma'am!
Yes, God!
Yes, HOMO!

All day!
All night!
Got house music poundin' in my brain.

Next question!
Yep, ya right.
I'm the weirdest Black man ya ever seen—

Deal with it.

THE END

hey, what

are you

looking for?

1. Earlier versions of all the poems in this collection have been shared on my Instagram accounts, @aedrane and @aedrane.poetry, between 2022 and 2025.

2. On Instagram, many of the poems in this collection have distinct color schemes, layouts, and formatting. I often use these elements to enhance the meaning behind the poem. In this book, I've edited many of the poems to better suit a black and white page. I also had to make some edits to accommodate limitations of the software I used to format this book. If you'd like a digital copy of *Gay Poem* with new and original designs in color, go to gaypoem.com/in-color.

3. "Suck It" was inspired by a quote from Elizabeth Bishop: "There's nothing more embarrassing than being a poet, really."

4. From Reddit posts, I borrowed the titles "Why Do Some Gay Men Hate Gay Men Who Are Feminine?" and "How the World Limits Us."

5. "How the World Limits Us" borrows from the chorus of "Never Enough" by Loren Allred. It also borrows *body-ody* from "Body" by Megan Thee Stallion.

6. "Stains" borrows *redrum* from *The Shining* by Stephen King and references "There's No Place Like Home" from the film adaptation of *The Wizard of Oz*.

7. "Hidden Folder Poetry" references "Still I Rise" by Maya Angelou. It also references *The Ethical Slut* by Janet W. Hardy and Dossie Easton.

8. I drew inspiration from Alok Vaid-Menon (@alokvmenon) for several lines in "Our Light." The line "you can put our bodies in a box and leave them out to rot on the side of the road," is a reference to the murder of Edwin Chiloba, a Kenyan fashion designer and LGBTQ+ activist. Initially, people suspected his murder was a hate crime. However, officials later reported that his murder was the result of intimate partner violence.

9. "Crumbs of a Constellation" borrows a quote from Quinta Brunson: "People be gay."

10. "Deal with It" references "Born This Way" by Lady Gaga.

11. The cover of *Yellowface* (2023) by Rebecca F. Kuang inspired the idea behind the cover design of this book. Ellie Game designed the cover of *Yellowface*.

ACKNOWLEDGEMENTS

This book started as a personal project on Instagram in 2022 and has since become one of the most fulfilling experiences of my life.

I will forever be grateful for all the people who have supported and encouraged me during the last three and a half years of working on the poems in this book. There were many times that I wanted to quit but didn't because of the messages and comments I received from people encouraging me to keep going. If you are one of those people, please know that I appreciate you more than I can put into words.

I'm also grateful for the Bangkok Lyrical Lunacy community. When I started writing poetry, I never imagined sharing my work in front of an audience of strangers. At my first Bangkok Poetry Slam, I was pleasantly surprised to find one of the most welcoming communities, making it possible for me to shine and build confidence in my voice and story. Special thanks to Pableroy for organizing and building such a wonderful community of lyrical lunatics.

I'm also grateful for the love and support from several of my closest friends throughout the creation of this book. Thank you Lisa Wills, John Lizcano, Ameer Sobhan, Aseem Afsah, Claudia Cruz Leo, Manuela Londoño Corrales, Maritza Bollain y Goytia, Peiley Lau, Michael Burns, Marli Gutierrez-Patterson, and Victor Montecinos.

Thank you to my therapist, Cherrie, for holding space for me in my darkest moments and helping me find an eternal light within myself. Thank you to every therapist I have ever worked with.

Thank you to the following people for contributing blurbs for this book: Gabriela Moriatry, Frederick Smith, Craig Casey Jr., Pablo Saba, Ryan Kull, Lisa Wills, and Nunoy van den Burgh.

Thank you, Gavin Bunyaratavej at Mango Tree Studios, for helping me record the *Gay Poem* audiobook. Thank you, Ark Saroj, for taking the photo of me included in this book. Thank you, Aaron McMillan, for helping bring to life the vision for this book's cover design.

Thank you to my mom, Sheba, for always loving me, encouraging me to be true to myself, and reminding me that I am destined to do great things. Thank you to my grandma, Dawn, for always loving me, supporting my dreams, and catching me every time I thought I was about to fall. Thank you also to my dad, my brothers, and everyone else in my family who never asked me to be anything other than me.

Thank you to my partner, Chew Meng Tham. Thank you for loving the fullest version of me, for being the first to read many of the poems in this book, for cheering me on at each live performance, for always helping to calm my neurotic mind, for constantly reminding me of my worth, and for never allowing me to give up on myself.

There may be some people who I've forgotten to include here, but please know you are not forgotten in my heart.

Thank you. Thank you. Thank you.

- Ameer Drane

www.ingramcontent.com/pod-product-compliance
Lightning Source LLC
Chambersburg PA
CBHW031449150726
47990CB00007B/2679